What people
Al Valdez and RISE UP NOW!

MW00415343

"Pastor Al has been a life-long friend and a brother. We have witnessed his transformation first hand to see the making of a man of God. He has overcome some of life's biggest challenges to become one of this generations great leaders. You will be inspired to become your best and reach your own personal potential…its your time to Rise Up Now!"

-Sonny Arguinzoni Jr.
Elder/Pastor Victory Outreach Church of Chino, CA

"You were created for greatness! In his new book, *Rise Up Now*, Al Valdez talks about how he defied all odds and found the strength to fulfill his destiny and realize his full potential. As he shares about his own journey, he offers a powerful message on how to protect and unlock the ultimate potential that is inside each of us. I encourage you to read this book. It will bring valuable knowledge that will help your personal growth and development, giving you courage, strength and hope to reach your full potential."

-Dr. Dave Martin
Speaker, Coach & Best-Selling Author of 12 Traits of the Greats

"Pastor Al is a leader, motivator, innovator and friend that comes around once in a generation. Through his vision and tireless efforts the Victory Outreach Urban Training Center was created which changed my life, opened my mind to a bigger vision, and more importantly taught me how to serve which was crucial in helping me become Compton's First Latino and youngest Council-member ever!"

-Isaac Galvan

Councilman District 2, City of Compton

"Al Valdez continues to exemplify true leadership and dedication in promoting community involvement. I have been fortunate to work directly with him and his passion to drive others to be their best is contagious and inspiring to those around him."

-Dena DiSarro

Executive Director of *One San Diego*

"I've experienced the ministry of my good friend Al Valdez for over fifteen years and I can truly say he knows the art of leadership, growth, and building a great organization. *Rise Up Now* is a must read for all upcoming leaders!"

-JAVEN

Gospel Artist & Host of TBN's *Praise*

"When I first met Pastor Al, I was remarkably impressed with how he engaged with the San Diego community. This is a direct reflection of the dynamic and outstanding leadership that Pastor Al provides to all he comes into contact with. I am honored and blessed to call Al Valdez a friend and brother in Christ."

-J.M. Hidalgo, Jr.
Sgt. Major (Retired) United States Marine Corp.
Republican Congressional Candidate/ Iraqi War Veteran

"Al Valdez has not only been a great personal friend for over twenty years, but he is also a true leader in his generation. From sharing the floor of a Brooklyn tenement building on an outreach to sharing international speaking platforms, I've had the privilege to watch him inspire others to be everything they were created to be. He's a proven pioneer and innovator and this book is packed full of insights on how to fulfill your potential in life."

-Paul Lloyd
Pastor/Author/Regional Leader
Victory Outreach Church of Manchester, England

LETS CONNECT!

For daily inspiration connect with Al Valdez on Social Media:

Instagram @al_valdez
Facebook @pastoralvaldez
Twitter @alvaldez

For weekly sermons on YouTube subscribe to:
Victory Outreach San Diego

Join our Victory Life Podcast on iTunes

For booking information contact Al Valdez at (619) 262-0172
www.vosd.tv

RISE

THE PATHWAY TO UNLOCKING

UP

YOUR PERSONAL POTENTIAL

NOW

Al Valdez

emerge

24 23 22 21 20 19   9 8 7 6 5 4 3 2 1

TULSA, OKLAHOMA

Published by:
Emerge Publishing, LLC
9521 Riverside Parkway, Suite 243
Tulsa, OK 74137
Phone: 888.407.4447
www.EmergePublishing.com

Library of Congress Publication Data
ISBN: 978-1949758-34-4 Paperback
ISBN: 978-1949758-35-1 E-book

BISAC Categories:
REL012070 RELIGION / Christian Living / Personal Growth
SEL027000 SELF-HELP / Personal Growth / Success
SEL044000 SELF-HELP / Self-Management / General

To my beautiful wife Georgina, we're making it count.

To Averi, Zanelle, Samara & Charisma,
never settle, reach for the best.

To my precious mother, Celia,
your prayers are working.

AJV, always in our hearts.

Contents

Special Acknowledgements

There is an African proverb that is not only simple but remains profound and true in my life. The proverb says, *"It takes a village to raise a child."* When I turned my life over to Jesus, I was that spiritual child, the ministry of Victory Outreach has been my village. Every village has a leader. Every family has a father and a mother. Pastor Sonny and Julie Arguinzoni have been my spiritual parents. From the very first day I met them, they have been a constant blessing in my life. Today we laugh together, we cry together, we have wonderful moments together as a family, but without their constant love, encouragement, support and exampleship, I am confident I would not be the leader I am today. Pastor Sonny has imparted many things into my life, not only through his words but through his example and assistance. The greatest thing I have ever learned from my pastors and mentors is that nothing is impossible with God. Because of that truth, Pastor Sonny has taught me the ability to believe and to bring out the best in others. God has certainly used him to bring out the best in my wife and I. For that I am eternally grateful.

Many years ago during the humble beginnings of Victory Outreach, God gave Pastor Sonny and Julie a promise found in the Bible. The book of Isaiah 45:2 & 3 reads, "I will go before you and make the crooked places straight; I will break in pieces the gates of bronze and cut the bars of iron. I will give you the treasures of darkness and hidden riches of secret places, that you may know that I, the Lord, who call you by your name, am the God of Israel." The promise is simple. God has a destiny and a vision for the so-called rejects of society. In those early days of the ministry God used them to reach and disciple the men and women who were rescued from their broken lives. What began as a small church in East Los Angeles, California expanded into many churches in different parts of the country and even other parts of the world.

By the time I walked into the church, Victory Outreach was already a world-wide ministry with thousands being reached. But the heart of Sonny and Julie continued to reach the unreachable, love the unlovable, and believe for the impossible. I certainly was that impossible case. The descendant of a broken family, a young man without hope and purpose, a fatherless youth as many of my generation were. I am grateful that they believed, and they saw something in me that I could not see within myself.

To walk with Sonny and Julie for 25 years is to walk with people who are true visionaries, people with a heart for the entire world. They eat, sleep, and speak vision every day of their lives. Their lives are contagious for God. Their impact on me has not only been profoundly positive, it has been more than that; their impact has changed the trajectory of my life and my family's future. Today Georgina and I assist them in leading and overseeing the ministry worldwide and we have the privilege of working closely with our heroes in the faith. The ministry of Victory Outreach International has celebrated 50 years, expanded to 30 nations of the world and to the depths of 3 generations. I honor my pastors, heroes and spiritual parents, under their leadership we have discovered our destiny and have thrived for God. Today, as we lead our churches and ministries we can believe because you first believed.

Your vision has become ours, the vision continues through us and we thank you for your faithfulness. I am grateful to be a descendant of this God given promise.

Isaiah 54:3, For you shall expand to the right and to the left, and your descendants will inherit the nations, And make the desolate cities inhabited.

Introduction

WHY I WROTE THIS BOOK

The journey of spiritual growth can sometimes be a frustrating experience. Have you ever been frustrated? Have you ever been discouraged? Have you ever just felt like you've been tapped out? I can remember being discouraged one day. On days like this I like to drive to the bookstore and spend a few hours walking around and reading books, hoping to take something home that will give me insight and provide valuable truth. Honestly, I have hundreds of books. Some of them I have read, some of them I have yet to get into, but books have always played a valuable role in my life development. On one such day, one small book piqued my interest. As I thumbed through it, I came across a story that impacted me. It is a story about the famous explorer, Sir Edmund Hillary.

Edmund Hillary was the first man to climb Mount Everest. On May 29, 1953, he scaled the highest mountain then known to man: more than 29,000 feet above sea level. He was knighted for his efforts and became an overnight sensation. In his book entitled, High Adventure, we find that Hillary had to grow into his success. You see, in 1952 he attempted to climb Mount Everest...but failed. A few weeks after his attempt, a group in England asked him to address its members.

Edmund Hillary walked on stage to thunderous applause. The audience was celebrating an attempt at greatness, but Hillary saw himself as a failure. He moved away from the microphone and walked to the edge of the platform. He made a fist and pointed at a picture of the mountain. He said in a loud voice,

"Mount Everest, you beat me the first time, but I'll beat you the next time because you've grown all you are going to grow...and I'm still growing!"

What a story! I wrote this book because every one of us has a mountain to climb. The mountain represents our personal potential. And when you and I were born, we were born with unlimited potential. Every one of us has been given a mind, a heart, dreams, ideas, gifts and abilities. Some of these things come naturally, other things are yet to be developed. But they are there and every one of us has been blessed by God with the ability to accomplish great things. However, we learn very quickly that nothing worthy happens overnight. It takes time to grow, it takes time to develop, it takes time to accomplish our dreams and visions. Like Edmund Hillary said, we are still growing. I can tell you that there are many books in my library that have been an incredible encouragement to me. Personal books that I keep as a reference through the years and lift me up. My prayer is that this book will do the same for you. I pray it becomes valuable to you in your life long journey of growth and development. There is unlimited potential in you.

Rise Up Now!

- AV

CHAPTER

1

DEFYING PERSONAL ODDS

"What doesn't kill you, only makes you stronger"

-FRIEDRICH NIETZSCHE

When I think of reaching our full potential in Christ, I can't help but think of my upbringing. I grew up 27 miles east of Los Angeles, California in a small town called Covina. But our family roots ran deep in the Boyle Heights section of East Los Angeles. My parents met at a very young age and were both products of a tumultuous family history. My father never knew his biological father because he abandoned the family when he was very young, leaving behind my grandmother to raise six children on welfare. They were very poor. My mother lost her father to drugs and alcoholism when she was 13 years old leaving behind my grandmother to raise four sons and a daughter by herself. They were also very poor and life in East LA was challenging. In those days, my father lost many friends to street violence and the war in Vietnam. My mother worked hard to finish high school but became pregnant with me at the age of 17.

> ### *My mother worked hard to finish high school but became pregnant with me at the age of 17.*

Many people in those days grew up fast and my parents were no exception. My father worked many odd jobs to try and support his young wife and newborn son. He did janitorial work, and took any job he could. I can remember that my mother worked for Winchell's Donut Shop. Things were tight financially. What I always admired about my father was his hard work ethic and his hunger for learning. Even though he was not formally educated, he was a very brilliant man. He was also able to move in different circles with different types of people. One day, he stumbled upon an opportunity with a friend and became an overnight success in business. He bought a house in Pico Rivera, California and eventually moved our family to Covina. He purchased a 4-bedroom house in a very nice area of the city and we even had a pool. He bought my Mom a brand new Z28 Camaro and he drove a brand-new Cadillac. Things were looking up. By that time, I had two brothers and every weekend our entire family would come from East LA to swim and party with the family. It was a time of great joy and the future looked bright. As the family began to grow and things got busy, it was clear that there were some unresolved issues in my parents' lives.

> ### In just a few years, my parents became an overnight success.

In just a few years, my parents became an overnight success. But what became abundantly clear was that they had not been healed of their own past and upbringing in East LA. Growing up without a father, carrying the pressure of family, struggling with their own personal demons, so to speak, all began to take a toll. My father began to drink and smoke marijuana every day. He wasn't very violent with us but with my mother it was another story. My mother, being so young, had the pressure of raising three crazy boys and she took a good job in the city. She eventually split from my father and moved back to East LA for a time. Meanwhile we stayed in Covina but things began to get very dark at home.

My parents worked hard to provide. My brothers and I were alone most days, all day. My father would drop us off at school in the morning, we would walk home after school, make something to eat and then get ourselves ready for baseball or football practice depending on the season. We would practice until dark and then ride our bikes home. Sometimes my father wouldn't be home, but sometimes he was. It didn't really matter. We had our own schedule. Even though my parents attempted to reconcile a few times, it never worked out. My parents divorced when I was 12 years old, right when I started Junior High School.

I was 12 years old the first time I smoked marijuana.

I was 12 years old the first time I smoked marijuana. We were hanging out at the baseball park when some older kids came up to us. We started playing handball and after hanging out for a while, they pulled out a joint. Honestly, I didn't feel pressured to smoke it. I had seen my father and uncles smoke weed my whole life and I was honestly curious to try it. So, I did. After that we would ride our bikes to the ballpark every day. It was our park and we did what we wanted.

Eventually, I started using drugs as often as I could and partying every chance I had. We started with marijuana, graduated to cocaine, and even did a lot of LSD; we tried it all basically. The City of Covina was predominately white, so being Mexican-American, we gravitated to the very few friends we could find with the same background. We learned to fight pretty early with other kids in the neighborhood, usually over racist comments or personal rivalries. Drugs were everywhere in those streets. As I got older and started attending high school, my house became a good place to party because my father was never home. My friends and I had it all to ourselves. We even had access to cars and started driving at the age of 14. Sometimes we would drive all the way down to Tijuana, Mexico for a good time, then just drive back. It was by the grace of God, we never got caught. We had some guns and would go shooting out in the desert. We had access to drugs and alcohol whenever we wanted. We were living the fast life early, but just like anything we eventually burned out. I was always good at sports, but that dream faded when I was kicked out of my first of five high schools for fighting. I tried out for the football team and made it to Varsity as a Sophomore, but was demoted to Junior Varsity because a teacher from my old school didn't like me and came to practice and spoke badly of me to the head coach. He said, I was a bad seed. Not having an engaged father in my life actually took a toll on me. I didn't really have the guidance I needed. I think back and wonder what opportunities I could have had if he was more available. But I suddenly realized, he grew up without a father and probably didn't really know what to do at that time. I don't hold anything against him for that. It was a vicious cycle that needed to be broken in our family tree. I have forgiven him and I am thankful for the short time I had with him in my life. My father passed recently, but I am grateful he was sober and drug free for over twenty years.

ENCOUNTERING CHRIST

On October 12th, 1993, I encountered Jesus Christ as my personal Lord and Savior. That evening, I knew that I would never be the same again. That evening, I knew I would never return to my old life and that I was ready to be made brand new. The seed of the gospel was planted deep in my life when I was just 9 or 10 years old. In the midst of our family's chaos as I described earlier, my mother exposed me to

Jesus. I can still remember one Easter morning she woke me up very early in the morning to attend a Sunrise Easter service at a local college. It was there that I heard the Good News for the very first time. I had never heard anything like that! As I started to attend Junior High School, I made many friends. Of all the friends I had through my school years, there was one who was not like everyone else. He was super charismatic, popular and we connected right away. What made him different than my other school buddies was that he was a P.K., a pastor's kid. I remember walking home from school one day and I asked him, "What kind of work does your dad do?" He said, "My dad has a church". Not really understanding anything about God or church, I ignorantly said, "Your Dad owns a church?" He said, "No, he is the pastor of the church. Maybe one day I will take you with me."

> ### *In the midst of our family's chaos, my mother exposed me to Jesus.*

When my buddy said, one day, he really didn't mean one day soon. The reason was that even though he was a pastor's kid, he was not serving God at the time. Tim was one of those kids in our neighborhood who we ran with in the streets. After we became friends in school, we did a lot together, and honestly, we were friends and partners in crime. We were young and foolish but we felt invincible. And we were having fun doing what we were doing.

Tim had an older sister named Georgina. She was actually the most popular girl in school. She was a grade older than us and she knew everybody, and everybody knew her. One day when I was walking home, I was passing our neighborhood McDonald's with a buddy and this beautiful fashionable young girl was hanging out with her friends, laughing and just owning the spot, she kind of called out and said, "Hey, are you Al Valdez?" I turned to her, paused and said, "Yeah that's me." She said, "You're friends with my brother Tim, right? He's been telling me about you, and I want to tell you something." I walked over to her and to be honest I was kind of nervous because I knew who she was and honestly, I was really struck by her. Let's just say, she had my full attention. She said, "Hey, there is a girl in school who thinks you're cute." I said, "Oh really? A friend?" She said, "Yeah." As she chewed her bubble gum, "A friend. I can introduce you tomorrow if you want. She really likes you." I said, "Ok. I'll meet her."

But here is the truth. I didn't need to meet that girl. The introduction was already made. From that day forward,

Georgina captured my heart. The next day, Georgina made the introduction with this girl, but I couldn't get my mind off of Georgina. Every day I went to school, the first thing I did was look for Georgina. I did all I could to be around her at school, the park and parties. I wanted to be where she was. For a teenage kid, I sure was acting whipped as we used to say in those days.

> **From that day forward, Georgina captured my heart.**

Georgina and I became a thing through high school. To be honest, our relationship was pretty rocky at times. I think it's because we were not serving God. As time went by we eventually split permanently after high school. We went our separate ways.

DARK TIMES

After Georgina and I split, times became very dark for me. I started to run with a group of friends who were heavily involved in drugs and violence. We all came from broken homes, we knew each other well and we had really no regard for our own lives. We spent our days thinking of new schemes, partying and getting into trouble all over the city of Los Angeles. We weren't officially a gang but we were a strong crew. Growing up in the Los Angeles area in the early 1990's, you had to be tough and alert. It helped to be "cliqued up" with the right people but it didn't always guarantee safety. Many of my friends had been shot, stabbed and even killed in those LA streets. But to us, it was an exciting life to live. We were young, we were strong and we felt invincible.

One night it was my turn. After running into an enemy at a backyard party, I confronted a person who had been looking for me. I knew I had to end the situation that night. So, as I confronted him, I grabbed him by his jacket and pulled it over his head, he immediately pulled out a knife. As we started to fight, he thrusted his knife at me, stabbing me in the chest right below my heart.

As the fight continued I felt the cold steel cut through my blue jeans on my right leg, and I pulled back realizing that he had a knife. He fell to the ground and I walked through the crowd that had gathered around us feeling victorious not realizing what had happened. I felt no pain, until a friend pointed to my chest and said, "You are bleeding!" They took me straight to the ER to get stitched up. I was lucky, after a night in the hospital and forty stitches later, I was back on my feet and back to my old ways.

I ran from God for almost two more years.

Friends, even though I had survived a violent stabbing, I ran from God for almost two more years. Truth is, on the outside I seem to be the same person, steelier in my resolve, more hardened by the street life. But on the inside, I was empty and hurting moving towards death and destruction. Life was like a fast-moving train, and I knew that the only way off was to jump!

TIME TO MAKE A CHANGE

At the young age of 19, I could feel that death was closer than life. I was not happy and there was an emptiness inside that I could not describe. One night I broke away from a party to find a telephone booth in my neighborhood. I picked up the phone and reached out to Georgina. When she answered the phone, my heart leaped. Hearing her voice was like the sound of fresh water flowing in a stream. It had been over a year since we had spoken and all the old feelings for her began to surface. Truth is the feelings never really left. As we exchanged our greetings, something sounded different in her voice. Honestly, it felt a little like she was waiting for my call. She began to tell me how good she felt and how well she was doing in life. I had heard through the grapevine that she had also faced some dark days, and was estranged from her own family for a while. But as she spoke, she spoke to me as if she was carrying some good news. I felt nervous as we spoke. The feelings of not hearing her voice for such a long time and the joy I sensed in her, all mixed with my own anxieties. I felt as if she was going to spring something on me that I was not ready to hear. She sounded as if she had found a relationship that made her very happy. She said, "Al, I want to tell you something." As I braced myself for what she was about to say, she declared, "I gave my life to Jesus, I am saved. I have been serving God for one year now."

When I heard her say these words, I can only describe my feelings to be something of relief. I was waiting to hear her say, "I found someone new." I mean, to me she sounded as if she was in a life-giving relationship that filled all of the emptiness inside of her. The truth is she had. She possessed the joy that only comes from an encounter with the Lord Jesus Christ. Upon hearing this good news, I wanted to choose my words wisely. In the past, Georgina and I had many conversations, sometimes heated, about God when we were dating, usually ending in the idea that I would never be a "church boy" or I didn't have a desire to be a Christian even though deep down she knew that God was calling her from a young age. Honestly, it seemed like serving God was something I could never really do. I loved the excitement of street life, partying, gambling, doing my own thing. In fact, I had scheduled a trip to Las Vegas for my approaching 18th birthday and I was ready to turn up! But, the pain of life was taking its toll on my heart. Mixed with the feeling of fear that began to plague me, I was convinced that death was close. Too many bad things were happening to me and around me, so I wanted to let Georgina know something about where I was spiritually. Right in that dark phone booth in my neighborhood, I said, "Georgina, don't count me out."

I took my broken life and willingly placed it into the hand of God.

It was only about one week later that I walked into Victory Outreach Church in La Puente, California. I saw young people just like me. Many of them grew up in my neighborhood, I felt at home. I also felt something that I had been missing for most of my life. I felt hope and I felt love. It didn't take me long to realize that the joy, peace and sense of purpose that I saw in these people was exactly what I needed. One month later, on a Wednesday night service, October 12, 1993, I quietly walked to the altar and gave my life to Jesus Christ as my personal Lord and Savior. On that day, I took my broken life and willingly placed it into the hand of God. It has turned out to be the greatest decision I have ever made, because on that day, Jesus not only saved me from a life of destruction, but he started me on a powerful journey of construction.

MAKE IT PERSONAL

Write your personal testimony. Take a glimpse into your life before Christ. (Use the chapter as a model.)

- What was my life like before receiving Christ?

  _____

  _____

  _____

  _____

- How did Jesus Christ come into my life?

  _____

  _____

  _____

  _____

- What is Jesus Christ doing in my life today?

  _____

  _____

  _____

  _____

CHAPTER

2

GOD'S PERSON

"Life is God's gift to a man,
what we do with it is our gift to God."

-A.R. BERNARD

It has been a great joy for my wife Georgina and I to have spent the last 25 years of our lives believing in people. Early on in our ministry, we accepted this calling. First working with youth, then working with college and career students, then pastoring a thriving church, and now working with leaders and pastors. Working with people is not easy, but there has never been anything more fulfilling than seeing someone reach their full potential. Someone once said, "Leaders are like bridges, they must be comfortable with people walking all over them." I have never had a problem with this quote, because I understand what it takes to develop people and help to launch them into their future. Our hopes would be that people would be willing to walk in the direction of God's will for their lives. Our prayer is that they rise higher than we ever could. We've spent many years of our lives working with people, and many have done well. What has brought success in their lives? It's very simple. When God's person submits to God's process, they become God's product. God knows exactly what He is doing with His people. He has already sealed and certified our future!

> **When God's person submits to God's process, they become God's product.**

Isaiah 46:10 NLT says, "Only I can tell you the future before it even happens. Everything I plan will come to pass, for I do whatever I wish". The New International Version says it this way, I make known the end from the beginning!"

This gives us hope because when it comes to God's way of choosing people, He never chooses the finished product, even though He sees the finished product in us. One of my good friends who has passed on used to say, "God is not looking for sharp tools, He is looking for tools to sharpen." When we talk about potential, understand that God sees something in you that you may not see you in yourself, but when you are God's person you must recognize that without God's shaping process, you cannot become God's product. Before I dive into the importance of "the process", I want to deal with "the person". Because a person who firmly understands his/her place in the Kingdom of God and firmly understands his/her place in God's plan will effectively navigate the process.

> **"God is not looking for sharp tools,
> He is looking for tools to sharpen."**

Recently, I was spending time with a young leader in my church who was gathering information for his college thesis. We began to discuss why some young people struggle in the church today. Together, we came to this conclusion. It is the problem of identity. Tragically, too many people have submitted to the world's idea of who they should be. Television, magazines, and the explosion of social media are all being used to craft and shape the identity of this generation. They are very powerful. I have spoken to many young leaders who struggle because they compare their lives to another person's life based on their social media highlights. Young leaders feel like they do not measure up because they seemingly don't have it all together. I have discovered that when people do not know who they are in Christ, they fail in God's process. Basically, they just quit. The first thing you are going to have to do in order to reach your potential is to recognize God's person is brand new.

I have a friend who owned a very large warehouse on a pretty rough piece of undeveloped land. He decided to put it up for sale because it was starting to require many repairs and upkeep that he could not afford at the time. He immediately started to get many inquiries about the property. Every time someone came to see the property he would envision them with ideas of what they could do with the warehouse equipment in order to turn a profit, and ideas on how they could refurbish the property. He even had some schematics drawn up for the buyers. One potential buyer came to see the property and after my friend began to give his usual pitch, the buyer interrupted him and said, "I appreciate all the work you have done, but I am only interested in buying the land this property sits on. When I see this land, all I see is potential for something like condominiums, a private school or an assisted living facility. I am working on a plan to knock down the warehouse and to build something brand new on the property."

When I think about this story, I can't help but think of the fact that God's plans for us are bigger and better than anything we could imagine. God is the ultimate developer! Through the sacrifice of Jesus Christ, our old life has been demolished with all of its defeats and failures and we have been given a new life with limitless potential. Through the blood of Jesus, we have been made brand new and it's time to start walking with a brand-new mentality.

Before you can say "hello" to your future, you must say "goodbye" to your past.

Someone said, "It's not the names they call you, it's the names you respond to that matter." Friends, before you can say "hello" to your future, you must say "goodbye" to your past. Here is what I have learned about potential. If you are still trying to fix the old person, you are working on the wrong thing. You are brand new.

We begin to struggle when we act like Christianity is just a better-behaved version of our old self. You are a new creation in Christ Jesus. I have met people with great potential who dwell too heavily on the past. And the truth is: There is nothing more useless than yesterday's newspaper. It is important to embrace the new thing that God is doing in your life. It's time to work on the new you. Let me break this down theologically. When you accepted Jesus, you were spiritually connected to everything that happened to Him on Calvary. God's person recognizes that the "old man" was crucified and buried with Christ. But, the new person has risen with Him. That is what baptism represents. It is an outward expression of an inward experience, a public statement. We are brand new.

"Therefore, if anyone is in Christ, he is a new creation; old things have passed away; behold, all things have become new." 2 Corinthians 5:17

What's new? We are given a brand-new name. We are no longer identified by the past. We are given a new heart. Our heart is no longer hard, it is tender. We are given a new disposition. We have no reason to be angry or contentious. We have joy, unspeakable and full of glory. We are given a new conscience. We have conviction. We can navigate right and wrong now. We have a new set of emotions. We have the fruit of the Spirit. We have a new destination. We have a heavenly destination. We are going somewhere and we are taking others along with us! We can dream big dreams and we can pray big prayers. You can dream again. You can visualize a great future!

GOD'S PERSON TAKES A STAND

Right off the bat you are going to have to take a stand on some things. The reason people of potential fall short is not only a lack of identity, but a weakness when it comes to people. Sometimes people are afraid of what others might think of them if they take a stand for God. So, they become people pleasers.

Young leaders are more worried about being liked than being effective.

What does this mean? Maybe young leaders are more worried about being liked than being effective. We are afraid that if we take a stand for our destiny, people will walk away from us, people will criticize us, people will stop being our friends, people will stop following us. There is a separation anxiety when it comes to people. Too many people of potential have fallen into the trap of people pleasing. So, we compromise our convictions over things that won't even matter in five years. Think about it.

When I was in high school, I quickly found out that image was so important. I can honestly say I spent way too much time worrying about my image, my clothing and the crowd I ran with. Everything in high school was about fitting in, who was most popular, who was the toughest, who was the best athlete, who was dating whom? Many students desired to fit in so badly they would do some pretty crazy things just to impress others.

Peer pressure really diverted me from God's plan for a long time. Truthfully, I was a follower at that time. I will tell you why. I can still remember as a Freshman, starting to drink beer with the Seniors. I thought that made me cool. I would stay out late at night on the weekends. I thought that made me cool. I would fight anyone who stepped in my face just to prove I was tough. I thought that made me cool. I would dislike someone just because an older kid told me to, when deep down I kind of liked the person. I thought that made me cool. I wanted to be accepted so badly. I can still remember being invited as a Freshman to a Halloween egg war where the Seniors would drive around town and throw eggs at the Freshman. Instead of bringing eggs, I brought a paintball gun and shot a bunch of Seniors with red paint balls. Now, I can't lie, it was pretty fun at the time but I was really lucky I didn't get arrested. I am sure we have all done things we aren't proud of in order to impress others, but here is my point. After all these years, none of those decisions matter in my life today. I don't even really talk to many high school friends today for whatever reason and the image that I was trying to create as a youngster is really kind of embarrassing to me. In other words, it doesn't matter anymore. It was a massive learning experience of how peer pressure diverted me from God's best for my life for a long season. What happens to our potential when we fall into the people pleasing trap? It could cause you to miss God's purpose for your life.

Here is the truth, we can't work on being what everyone else wants us to be and what God wants us to be at the same time. The good intentions of people can take you off track if you are not careful. I have discovered that young leaders of today live between two realities, envy and peer pressure.

ENVY AND PEER PRESSURE

Many young people are either trying to copy someone else or following some trend, or, they are being pressured into doing things that they were not called to do for themselves. The result is that frustration sets in and they can stall out. They give valuable energy to a path that is not for them. I have seen how later in life they can become frustrated because they become a slave to someone else's idea for their life. It is important to know what God has called you to do. A friend of mine who is a pastor says, "Too many people spend their life building only to realize they built upon the wrong foundation."

It can even happen in marriage. One thing I love about my wife is that she has always kept a sincere reverence for my calling and God's plan for my life, and I have always kept a reverence for God's plan for her. We are very sensitive to each other's identity, dream and conviction. We have determined in our hearts that we will not pressure each other into being and doing something that is outside of God's will for us as individuals, primarily because we have spent many years praying and seeking God for His plan. In other words, we know who we are in Christ and we respect that about each other.

But when people are BIG in our lives, God's power becomes diminished.

Secondly, peer pressure prevents you from growing your faith. Faith plays an important factor in developing your potential. When God is BIG in our lives, people have less power to lead us in the wrong direction. But when people are BIG in our lives, God's power becomes diminished. It affects us. It hinders and shifts our dependency. The challenge is, we give to people what belongs to God and give to God what belongs to people. God and people cannot be the same size in your life. There must be an order. The question is where do you place your faith? Is your faith in man or is your faith in your Heavenly Father?

John 5:44 says, "No wonder you can't believe! For you gladly honor each other, but you don't care about the honor that comes from the one who alone is God. "(NLT)

People of potential know how to spend time with God in prayer. They know that God is the ultimate giver of strength and power. They know that the vision originates in the heart of God and is graced to the heart and minds of men and women. They know how to kneel before God for their future.

And one thing I have learned is that when we kneel before God, we can stand before anyone when obstacles arise.

People of potential know how to spend time with God in prayer.

Finally, peer pressure can lead you to hypocrisy and sin. Understand me when I say you will never be able to please everyone. Pleasing causes people to put on a "mask". They become one thing in front of one group of people and something else in front of another group. But when people try to please everyone they will eventually give in to the pressure. When this happens, they can be led into sin. Pressure challenges our character. For some, pressure can cause some to compromise what they truly believe and do things that are contrary to God's Word. Pressure causes immature leaders to do strange things. Be careful to be a pleaser of God even when it causes you to be unpopular.

PEOPLE WHO WERE PRESSURED

There are some clear examples in scripture of what pressure does to people. Pilate was pressured by the crowd to crucify Jesus. Peter was pressured to deny Christ three times. Joseph's brothers conspired and pressured each other to sell Joseph into slavery. Nobody spoke up. Nobody had the courage, nobody had the backbone. You'll never reach your potential with a "wishbone". It can only be reached with a "backbone". Ten spies were pressured by each other and defeated the whole nation of Israel with a negative report! Pressure literally stopped an entire nation from reaching the promised land. What God wanted to do, had to wait forty years, because they did not know who they were or whose they were. They did not understand the powerful potential they possessed. Pressure kept them out of the promised land instead of moving into the promise. They basically missed out because of the fear that permeated the camp.

As we grow in God's plan, you will discover that spiritual growth is not an overnight process. Just like anything great in this world, a life of excellence takes time to develop, positive resistance to strengthen, and forward movement to advance. Keep your eyes on your spiritual goals and dig deep. Recognize the journey and stay in submission to your God given goals. Identify the people in your life that help to keep you focused versus those who have a tendency to divert you. Know the difference and take a strong stand for Jesus! Watch what God is able to do in your life!

MAKE IT PERSONAL

- "God knows exactly what He is doing with His people." Do you understand what it takes to be developed ? What does this quote mean to you?

_____

_____

_____

- "When Gods person submits to Gods process they become Gods product." What does submitting to Gods process look like to you in this season.

_____

_____

_____

- In reference to Isaiah 46:10 the author states this gives us "hope". Have you ever felt hopeless in a situation , task or challenge?

_____

_____

_____

_____

- "God sees something in you " Can you recall a moment when you couldn't see it in yourself?

  _____

  _____

  _____

- Identify where God is doing a new thing in your life.

  _____

  _____

  _____

- Can you recall a specific time when your balance was off and pleasing people was taking over.

  _____

  _____

  _____

- What tries to pressure you? Any incidences when you experienced peer pressure?

  _____

  _____

  _____

- Personal Application: Write in your own words some things you want to apply from this chapter.

  _____

  _____

  _____

  _____

CHAPTER

3

GOD'S PROCESS

*"Trust the process, we always end up
right where we are meant to be,
right when we are meant to be."*

-ANONYMOUS

Think about this for a moment. Whenever someone in
scripture asked God for a destiny, He assigned them a
challenge, a wilderness, so to speak. I can't help but think
about Moses and the Children of Israel in the desert, David
in the shepherd's field, and many others who God called
but also placed in a process for their spiritual development.
To me, the premiere example of how God develops a
person for his plan and harvests full potential in a person's

life is Joseph. When God gave Joseph his vision, he was 17 years old and he was very immature. Fast forward thirteen years later, we find a very different man. Along his journey of development, Joseph had been stripped of his colorful coat, thrown into a pit, sold into slavery by his brothers and that was just the beginning. There were a whole lot of events that happened in Joseph's life before he was elevated and promoted.

Joseph endured some difficult and unfair hardships. But every struggle, every test, every trial was designed to prepare and mature Joseph to be the full grown spiritual adult God desired him to be. In the end, God used Joseph greatly to save and preserve his people. The bottom line is, God could trust him because he endured the process of spiritual development in his life. The purpose of the process is to take us from infancy to maturity. Joseph needed the process because he would not have been effective in the place God wanted him to be, had he remained a spiritual infant. This is a problem we see in the church today. Churches are spiritually ineffective because the leadership has not allowed God to take them through a process of development. More and more leaders are ineffective today because they have not allowed the fire of God to test them. They are talented but they are not tested. They are gifted but they have not grown. They are passionate but they are under-prepared. They have not been weaponized by the process. Therefore, they are not very effective. Above anything in our lives, God desires to grow our character.

> ### God doesn't use us according to our age, He uses us according to our spiritual maturity.

What did the gospel writers say about spiritual growth? Hebrews 5:12-14 says, "For though by this time you ought to be teachers, you need someone to teach you again the first principles of the oracles of God; and you have come to need milk and not solid food. For everyone who partakes only of milk is unskilled in the word of righteousness, for he is a babe. But solid food belongs to those who are of full age, that is, those who by reason of use have their senses exercised to discern both good and evil." The gospel writers make a very clear distinction between spiritual childhood and spiritual adulthood. And here is the challenge, some think they are adults while they act like children, and some think of themselves like children when they are actually supposed to be adults. Clearly, God doesn't use us according to our age, He uses us according to our spiritual maturity. In developing our potential, it is not enough to know about the process, it is also important to know where you are in the process. In my time of developing people of potential, I have discovered four spiritual levels in the process. Take some time to think of where you might be in the process of spiritual development.

LEVEL ONE: SPIRITUAL CHILDREN

These are the babes in Christ. We have all passed through this phase, it is a requirement. Nicodemus was very intuitive and asked Jesus how he could be saved. Jesus said, "Unless one is born again, he cannot see the kingdom of God." When you were born again, you were transferred out of an old kingdom into a new kingdom. You left as whatever you were in that old kingdom and you came in as a newborn child. Whatever you were in the darkness, you are no more, and what you become in the light is a spiritual babe in Christ. I know this sounds funny, but when we are born again, we become babies. What is a baby? A baby is dependent for everything. Nobody expects a baby to get from the hospital to the home without the help of the family. Babies are very fragile. My oldest daughter Averi is 21 years old, but I can still remember what it felt like to bring her home from the hospital. My wife Georgina and I were super nervous. Now we had the responsibility of taking care of a little life that would depend on us for everything. I think deep down if I could have found a way of raising her in the hospital I would have. After all, what did I know about raising children? But it was obvious to me that a child grows best in a healthy family environment. It was the slowest and most careful drive home I ever made. And we have experienced the joy and pain of raising children.

What do spiritual babies need?

They need certain food. They can't just eat anything. They can't handle it because they have not developed their little teeth. They need milk in order to be nourished spiritually.

1 Peter 2:2, "Therefore laying aside all malice, all deceit, hypocrisy, envy, and all evil speaking, as newborn babes, desire the pure milk of the word, that you may grow thereby..."

Babies can't feed themselves. Babies rely on their parents ability to feed them. From a spiritual standpoint, new believers rely on our teaching, our word and our example. They need special care and attention. They are very fragile. We are more careful around babies, aren't we? We must be careful how we do things when a baby is around.

Also, babies must be carried. The business of carrying babies is a billion-dollar industry. There are so many instruments you can find for carrying and mobilizing children. Clearly our spiritual children are no different. When it comes to being a "spiritual child", I can only think of the people God sent into my life to feed me spiritually, care for me, coach me and to sometimes carry me. What is amazing, is that those people are still in my life today! I am so grateful for those who saw my potential early on. I try to express my gratefulness to them as often as possible. Why? Because they spent valuable time and energy investing into my spiritual life and took the time to help me build a strong foundation in Christ.

Level Two: Spiritual Teenagers

I have raised two teens and I am raising two more, as I write this book. Let's just say, teenagers are at a very unique and seemingly strange phase of life. They are actually going through a metamorphosis: not quite a man, not quite a boy; not quite a woman, not quite a girl but something in between, spiritually speaking. One thing I have discovered from raising two teenagers myself, everything with a teenager is about struggle. I have seen how my two teens have struggled with the ups and downs of their emotions.

Teens struggle with their minds, they struggle with their identity, they struggle with their bodies, they struggle with their relationships, they struggle with their attitude, the key word is struggle!

WHAT DO SPIRITUAL TEENAGERS NEED?

Teenagers need direction. Why? Because they are still discovering their God-given identity. Teens are still trying to find themselves. They have a tendency to search things out, they have exploring minds. They are forming ideas about the world in which they live. They are open to new things. They often think the latest thing is the greatest thing. But, direction keeps them on the right track spiritually.

"It's easier to raise a child than to repair an adult."

Teenagers also need correction. Teens are going to make mistakes in their lives, because they desire to test the limits. They need some strong examples who will be willing to bring correction in love. Teens need someone who will point out their mistakes and help them develop into the person God has called them to be. Although their body language doesn't show it, deep down they desire correction because it tells them you care about them! It tells them you believe in them. This has been something I had to learn. Truthfully, I have discovered there are two ways to deal with teens, ignore them or raise them. Raising spiritual children is hard work, but if we fail to step in, we risk crooked development. Someone once said, "It's easier to raise a child than to repair an adult."

Thirdly, they need patience, understanding and support. In one conversation with my teenage daughter, we discussed how many of her friends in school need spiritual support in their lives. They have hopes and dreams, but really lack someone who can help them along the way. We talked about how so many are put down by people they admire on a daily basis and are looking for someone to believe in them personally. This requires the patience of a mentor. Patience is required in the person doing the developing and patience is required in the person being developed. When someone with patience and understanding steps into a teens life, the possibilities are limitless in that person. People need someone to believe in them, encourage them and keep them excited about their future. I have discovered that people will go much farther than they ever thought they could, because someone else thought they could. If you find yourself hungry for direction, look for a mentor or a model who is moving in the direction you desire to go! And be sure to cultivate a strong relationship along the way!

Level Three: Spiritual Adults

The third level of spiritual development is spiritual adulthood. From a practical standpoint, an adult is someone who has been through a process in their life and that process has taught them to be responsible and mature. I love what Paul the Apostle said to the Corinthian church.

1 Corinthians 13:11, "When I was a child, I used to speak like a child, think like a child, reason like a child; when I became a man, I put away childish things."

1 Corinthians 14:20, "Dear brothers and sisters, don't be childish in your understanding of these things. Be innocent as babies when it comes to evil, but be mature in understanding matters of this kind."

What makes adults powerful is that adults have goals, adults have dreams, but adults are not doing things only for themselves. They understand that they are only a small part of a bigger plan. Adults have taken on spiritual responsibilities and they have children they must care for. They recognize that a wise person leaves an inheritance for their children. And if they don't have children, they have responsibilities that are directly linked to the next generation. Today our ministry has growth to its breadth because of men and women who have grown up to take full responsibility for the work of God. Now, spiritual adults are in the physical and spiritual position to lead, and the world becomes disappointed with adults who do not take their place. Here is what I have learned, when you are an adult, you go higher in the process, but your margin for error becomes smaller. What is expected from adults? First, excuses are no longer heard. Second, errors are judged more harshly. Third, excitement is no longer the motivation. A spiritual adult is motivated by purpose and that purpose gives them excitement. When they see results, they gather strength to carry on and to move ahead in spite of the circumstances. What are some key characteristics of spiritual adulthood.

First, adults eat differently. Where babies drink milk, teenagers can pretty much eat anything they want and not gain weight. Adults need the meat of God's word to gain growth and strength for the task. Where children are dependent and fed, and teens try anything, adults determine their diet by conscious choice. They are more wise and more selective in what they take in and that is what makes them strong. Also, adults are developing self control. They can rule their lives effectively. They do not always require outside motivation. They are vision driven, self-motivators, they move with character and conviction in their lives.

**_Prov. 25:28, "A person without self control
is like a city with broken down walls."_**

The next point is very important. Adults accept responsibility for the family. They are leaders in marriage, leaders when raising kids, they learn to manage life's affairs well; they are responsible with money, the house, the dog, their job, the lawn, their personal goals and every other responsibility linked to success in their lives. Here is the point, for the adult, there is nobody to blame. The buck stops with them. They are willing to take responsibility and increase what God has entrusted them with. Lastly, adults are generous. They know how to passionately give. I think one of the things I have learned in my life is that God desires to develop me into a person of significance. Today my life is dedicated to lifting up the lives of others and I have learned to be generous in every area that I can.

When I have been generous with my time, I have reaped friendships, when I have been generous with my gifts, I have reaped great joy and have seen others lifted, when I have been generous with my finances, I have reaped finances in return. Giving has become a very important part of my lifestyle.

What does the Bible say about giving? Well, first the word of God promises favor.

Proverbs 18:16, "A gift opens the way and ushers the giver into the presence of the great."

Secondly, the Bible promises abundant blessing to those who practice generosity.

2 Corinthians 9:8, "And God is able to bless you abundantly, so that in all things at all times, having all that you need, you will abound in every good work."

In conclusion, when Joseph was finally elevated to the right hand of Pharaoh, he had experienced many challenging things within his life that shaped him into the man he had become. Instead of executing punishment and revenge on the brothers who tried to kill him and sold him into slavery, Joseph does something that gives us insight to what it means to fulfill our potential. Joseph forgave his brothers. We see this unfold in Genesis 50:15-21. When his brothers were rightfully afraid to approach him after they had done all those horrible things to him. Joseph wept and placed no blame on them for their hate, anger and jealousy. Joseph acknowledged God's process in his own life, and because of his relationship with God, he knew that God only used those circumstances to develop him into the spiritual adult he had become!

Joseph also made a commitment to take care of his brothers who had fallen on hard times. Joseph accepted the role and responsibility of caring for and preserving his family bloodline. The dream that God had given him when he was merely 17 years old had finally come to pass. He had been elected by God for a powerful purpose. And that purpose was to rescue his family and his people so that they could endure for the future. Ultimately, Joseph had become a full grown spiritual adult. Joseph started as a loud mouth young man, full of pride and arrogance and through the process became a strong spiritual adult who could carry the weight of responsibility given to him by God himself. He is proof that when we submit to God's process in our lives, we can also develop into men and women who can carry the weight of responsibility in our lives. If you find yourself in God's process today, I want to encourage you to stay in the fight. God is shaping you into a powerful vessel for Him. As we grow, God uses us in a way that we could never imagine!

MAKE IT PERSONAL

- Who is God using to help you repair the crooked areas in your life?

_____

_____

_____

- What spiritual level do you see for yourself?

_____

_____

_____

- Identify times when you felt like you were in the wilderness? Like Joseph, what test does God want you to pass in order to build trust with him?

_____

_____

_____

- Are you in a life group? What avenues are you taking to develop from one level to the next (babies, teens, adulthood) What are tools that you have been given?

_____

_____

_____

Personal Application: Who do you give permission to speak into your life? Ask them if there are areas in your life where you need to grow in order to move to the next level.

Be intentional, you're your process.

CHAPTER

4

THE WILDERNESS EXPERIENCE

"The LORD your God led you all the way in the wilderness these forty years, to humble and test you in order to know what was in your heart..."

-DEUTERONOMY 8:2

One of the many things I love about God is that He is a risk taker. I have found that God is not afraid to choose a leader before his time. He anointed David as King when he was just a teen. He chose Samuel as a boy when he was serving in the temple. He also chose Esther to become Queen of Persia at just fourteen years old. God loves using young people. God will choose a young man or woman before their time and then just sit back and watch them grow. The process is God's way of developing us into the leaders He has called us to be.

God is not afraid to choose a leader before his time.

I can still remember when Georgina and I responded to the call of God to enter into the ministry. We were recently married and were very young. I was just 23 years old. We were both saved in the ministry of Victory Outreach at the age of 19. Growing up in Los Angeles, CA, we felt a passion to reach and serve young people, like ourselves, through our local youth ministry. We had a bible study with about 50 kids and a drama that traveled around the country that was reaching young people and making a strong impact in young lives. We had just recently returned from doing a very successful evangelistic crusade in New York City, when one day we received a phone call to meet with our pastor, Pastor Sonny Arguinzoni, Founder of Victory Outreach International.

In that meeting, our pastor began to express an idea that he had to open up a training center for young people who had been ignited by the Holy Spirit and had a desire for ministry training and exposure. He envisioned young people from all over the world who would travel to the training center for spiritual separation, evangelism training and ministry exposure. He asked us if we would be willing to go and develop this ministry with his guidance and support. To be honest, at that very moment I felt very nervous and excited at the same time. I think, whenever you are asked to do something for God, there is a feeling of inadequacy and a lack of self-confidence. But without really knowing what I was saying, I blurted out "Yes. Pastor. We are willing to go." His response was, "Good!" I asked him, "When would you like us to go?" He said, "Right away. We already have a building and a church that will help as a base for the students." My next question was the question that hit me in a way that maybe I wasn't so prepared for. I asked him, "Where will the training center be built?" He said, "We have a facility in Bridgeport, Connecticut. We will build it there." My next thought was...

...''Where in the world is, Bridgeport, Connecticut?''

In just a matter of a few weeks, along with my wife and our newborn daughter, we traveled 2,850 miles by car to one of the poorest cities in America. Bridgeport, at that time was one of the most violent, drug infested cities in America.

Coming from a largely Mexican-American community in Los Angeles to a multi-cultural and truly urban environment in Bridgeport was culture shock, to say the least. From the weather, to the music, to the food, to the people, everything was so different from what we were used to. As we pulled up to the facility at 381 Jane St., we had our first glimpse of the large house and were pretty amazed to see that the streets surrounding the building were full of people from the neighborhood, but the streets were also barricaded with cement barricades to stop drug dealers from driving straight down the street and to prevent drive-by shootings. It was somewhat of a maze. We found that many of the tenement buildings had been burnt by fire. Some were being used as shooting galleries and crack-houses.

The training center was an old Catholic Rectory given by the Diocese of Bridgeport to Victory Outreach International for our use. It needed work and repairs which we were happy to do. The first night in the UTC (as we call it today), was filled with the sounds of mice in the walls, loud voices in the neighborhood, and machine gun fire in the streets. This would be the place where God would begin my journey of personal development and for hundreds of young leaders who would walk through the doors of that facility over the next 20 years.

WHAT IS THE WILDERNESS EXPERIENCE?

During those early days in Bridgeport, I came face to face with the need for spiritual development within my own life. I could remember thinking, "How can I lead these young potential leaders spiritually, if I have yet to grow so much?" We set out to develop a spiritual path for the students who arrived at the Urban Training Center. It was here that they would spend six months to one year of their lives with us. We woke up early in the morning for prayer at 6 a.m. We spent hours traveling and working the sin-filled East Coast streets ministering to young people, drug addicts and anyone who would listen. Many times, we would invite people to our house for a hot meal and a shower. The work was very exciting. We witnessed the power of God move in people's lives, but to be honest the work was very difficult. There were many times of discouragement and weakness in my own life. The streets of New York City, Philadelphia and Newark, New Jersey have a way of testing your resolve.

I can remember one day in particular. Every Tuesday, we would drive two hours from Bridgeport, Connecticut to Brooklyn, New York by invitation from a pastor who was pioneering a small church in the city. We would often spend the entire day and night hitting the streets and holding outdoor street rallies in the city. That night we would be inviting people into the church for a church service that we would be conducting that evening. Having spent many weeks working those Brooklyn streets in the cold fall weather (New York gets cold around that time), we hadn't seen much of a response from the people. The city is fast. The people were tough and tender and it really took time to get a breakthrough. Let's just say my hopes were not very high for a successful event. So, as we entered the church sanctuary with about thirty students, we set out to pray before we hit the streets. I knelt down to pray in one of the hard church pews. After a long period of time which actually seemed pretty short, I felt a gentle tap on the shoulder as I kneeled in the pew. It was the pastor of the church. What he said to me sort of shocked me and left me a bit confused. He asked, "Are you OK?" I said, "Yes, I am good." As I looked around, I noticed that everyone was gone. I asked, "Where are all the students?" He said, "They all went to the streets, you fell asleep during prayer. But I figured you needed the rest."

I was pretty embarrassed. I was supposed to be their fearless leader. But here I was sleeping in the church pew. Looking back, I can honestly say that in those days God was more interested in building me before we could start building anyone else. I have learned that it is not the ministry that makes the man, it is the man who makes the ministry and God uses the wilderness to develop us. Be encouraged if you are having a wilderness experience.

Lack and Learning

I may not know what your wilderness looks like today, but I can be sure that whatever it may be, God's purpose is to develop you into the person He has called you to be. The wilderness is a special time in a leader's life.

First of all, it is a time of loneliness. Many have studied the life of a young leader named David. David was anointed to be King of Israel at the tender, young age of 16 years old. And when the prophet Samuel was sent by God to the house of Jesse, Samuel almost missed it. As Jesse presented seven of his sons before the prophet, Samuel saw seven perfectly groomed men who looked ready for the task. But what Samuel saw on the outside, only God could see on the inside.

But the Lord said to Samuel,

"Don't judge by his appearance or height, for I have rejected him. The LORD doesn't see things the way you see them. People judge by outward appearance, but the LORD looks at the heart." 1 Samuel 16:7 (NLT)

59

God then directed Samuel to ask Jesse if he had another son, and we know that Jesse's eighth son was tending his father's sheep in the shepherd's field.

Like David, many leaders must endure a season of loneliness.

Tending sheep is not an easy task. I don't imagine David, the youngest son of Jesse, enjoying the job of taking care of smelly sheep. I can imagine a young dreamer/visionary in the making having to wake up early in the morning, work hard to corral and lead the sheep to green pastures, protect the sheep, and clean and care for the sheep all the while keeping his eyes fixed on his passions and his dreams for the future! Like David, many leaders must endure a season of loneliness. Loneliness is a time where God tests our hearts and teaches us to walk alone while never taking our eye off of the task He has given us. Leadership is not a popularity contest. In fact, the higher God begins to raise up a leader, the more unpopular leadership can be because of the tough stands and decisions a leader must make in order to protect and guide the people he leads. The wilderness experience teaches a leader how to stand in those times! David began with humble work and eventually God moved him to a high position. He chose David, his servant and took him from the sheep pens; from tending the sheep he brought him to be the shepherd of his people Jacob, of Israel his inheritance.

"And David shepherded them with integrity of heart; with skillful hands he led them."

Psalms 78:70

LEARNING TO TRUST BY FAITH

The wilderness experience is also a time of lack. In the English dictionary, the word lack means, "the state of being without or not having enough of something." Having endured a wilderness experience in my own life, I can say it was a beautiful time of faith building for me. The wilderness experience is a time where a young leader learns to trust God for everything! For my wife Georgina and I, we had to learn to trust God to adjust to being far away from our family and home church. We had to trust God for personal development and ministry growth in a difficult region. We had to trust God for financial provision for a pioneering ministry. We had to trust God for pretty much everything else. But the exciting truth is that God always came through for us in every situation.

"We are totally out of money."

I can remember one of the first times I experienced God's provision for our ministry. We were set to go to Boston, Massachusetts with our training center students for an evangelistic crusade. The pastor in Boston at the time was pioneering a work and requested our traveling drama ministry. We were believing for many young people to get touched by God and saved that weekend. The night before we were scheduled to drive up to Boston, our office administrator called me in to give me some bad news. She basically said, "We are totally out of money." In those early days, it was pretty challenging to feed, house and clothe thirty plus students on a daily basis. Many of our students at the time came from broken families and some were newly saved. They depended on the financial support of church friends. So, let's just say we were all learning to trust God.

I kept the news at heart and I figured I had a few days to figure things out. Feeling a little stressed, I went upstairs to say goodbye to Georgina and Averi before I left for the weekend to Boston with the students. After a long hug and prayer, Georgina said, "I don't want to stress you out, but Averi only has enough diapers left for the weekend. Can you leave me a few dollars so I can get a few more?" I said, "Of course." We packed up the vans and off we went to Boston.

God moved in a powerful way in Boston! For two days, we saw hundreds fill the Strand Auditorium to hear the gospel through our drama ministry. It was amazing to see literally 200 to 300 young people surrender their lives to Jesus! I can honestly say that our days on the East Coast were some of the most powerful and fulfilling times in our early ministry.

As we were getting ready to make our way back to Connecticut, the pastor of the church asked to take me out to a quick lunch before I left. We rejoiced over the events of the weekend and talked about the great things God did in the people's lives. As our lunch came to an end, the pastor wished to thank me for our ministry time and took out a check to give me for some of our ministry expenses while we were there in Boston. As the pastor reached out to give me the envelope, for the first time, I felt the Holy Spirit in a way I never had. I sensed that God didn't want me to take that check. During our time, I could see how the church was pioneering and how many sacrifices the pastor and his family were making to reach that city for Jesus. I sensed that he might need those resources to follow up on the people we had reached and to continue to build the church. But the truth was, I also had a need at the training center. We had just enough gas for our return, we were running short on many things at the house and our bills were stacking up. But nevertheless, I felt God telling me not to take that check.

The pastor insisted I take the check. After a short struggle, I agreed to take it. Then, I looked the pastor in the eye and said, "Pastor, I am humbly asking you to receive this check. I feel I need to sow another seed into your church, because I am trusting God for something in my life by faith." With those words, he reluctantly agreed and gladly received the seed. After that lunch, I felt a powerful release. I felt I had been obedient to the Holy Spirit as He was prompting me to sow into that church. But the challenges remained back at home.

> **For the first time, I witnessed the power of generosity in my life.**

When we arrived back in Bridgeport, we were excited about the things that took place in Boston and for the first time, I witnessed the power of generosity in my life. Our office administrator was so excited to greet me with the news. She pulled my wife and I into the office and said, "You will never believe this! We just checked the mail, and there is check for the training center in the amount of $10,000 dollars!" We were shocked. We had never seen that much money before. All of our needs were met and we had some money to spare for van repairs and other building needs. God just blew our minds! We later found out that our pastors wife, Julie Arguinzoni was secretly raising funds for our ministry on the East Coast and she continued to be a great blessing to us while we served out there.

Two days later, I received a call from Boston. It was the pastor. He said, "I want you to know how much of a blessing you were when you were here in Boston. In a few days, I am sending you a package." The next day, a mail truck pulled up to the training center. The mail man asked, "Where can we unload this?" I asked, "What is it?" He said, "It looks like a year's worth of baby diapers." I learned a valuable lesson about faith that week. When you listen to God's voice and are willing to grow in seasons of lack, God will always come through and trust you with more in your life.

THE UNIVERSITY OF ADVERSITY

The wilderness experience is a time of learning. We all know that it is important to educate ourselves to the highest degree. Information is an important part of growth, but it is equally important to mix experience with learning. Every leader will eventually have to enroll in a school called, The University of Adversity. Some might even call it the School of Hard Knocks.

When we think of adversity, we often think of opposition to our mission or the obstacles we must learn to overcome in order to be successful. However, might I also present to you that failure is an essential part of growth in our lives. Now, I'm not speaking of moral failure or scandalous character breakdowns that sometimes cause a young leader to lengthen their wilderness and hurts people along the way. But, I am speaking of the failure we experience when stepping out by faith! This is God's way of teaching us to be great for His glory.

There are many examples of failures in the Bible. Men and women who experienced adversity in their attempt to do great things for God. Moses was a failure. He attempted to deliver the children of Israel the wrong way, when he killed a man in anger. Peter was a failure when he attempted to walk on water and sank because he took his eyes off of Jesus and focused on the storm. Paul was a failure when he attempted to preach the gospel in Lystra. He was stoned and dragged out of the city considered dead, but after he was strengthened by his fellow disciples, he rose again and eventually won the city for Jesus. Time and again we see leaders who have failed at trying something new or attempting something great, but they were eventually successful because of their resilience and passion.

You see, that is what leaders do, they take the hits but they get back up to fight another day! They overcome adverse circumstances. They climb over personal challenges and complexities. They push through bad seasons. They take their eyes off of the attack and focus on the assignment. And they experience the breakthrough! Moses failed but he eventually delivered God's people from Egypt. Peter failed but he eventually preached the first sermon and thousands were saved and the church was birthed. God used Paul to spread the Good News throughout the known world! Adversity was their greatest teacher. Adversity did not defeat them, adversity shaped them for greatness and harvested their potential! In my personal experience, there are three ways adversity grows our lives and harvests our potential.

The Benefits of Adversity

First, adversity brings us closer to God. There is nothing that will build the prayer life of a true believer like a personal storm. I like to call these types of storms, "correcting storms". Sometimes adversity is from outer sources but sometimes storms are self-inflicted through inner forces and wrong behavior. When a storm is self-inflicted because of sin, Satan will use the storm to bring discouragement in the hopes of getting us to quit, but God will use the ensuing storm to bring us back to His love and mercy. God will not hesitate to use our personal circumstances to teach us to pray and to rebuild our relationship with Him through prayer. I believe that the storm can never get the best of a praying man or woman. Catch this: What the enemy uses to take you out, God uses to take you up! God will use our personal circumstances to bring us closer to Him. Storms teach us to pray and seek God.

Adversity brings us closer to the people that God desires to grow us and perfect us for His plan.

Secondly, adversity brings us closer to people. These are called "perfecting storms". Adversity brings us closer to the people that God desires to grow us and perfect us for His plan. As Christians, we are not called to walk alone. Not only do we have the Holy Spirit in our lives, we also have the people of the church to lean on when times are difficult. The church is a family filled with victorious believers who can relate with the challenges we face on our way to becoming what God has called us to be. The enemy's plan is to use adversity to divide people and to isolate the believer, but God uses adversity to bring us closer together, especially in tough times. I've seen and experienced for myself how storms can bring us closer to our loved ones and closer to people because of compassion and love. God uses His people to strengthen, coach and disciple us towards Jesus Christ.

Finally, adversity brings us closer to our purpose. These are what I call "directing storms". The greatest example I can use for this point is the prophet Jonah. God called him to go to Nineveh to preach and warn the people of coming destruction. Jonah was called to preach repentance so that God would not destroy the city. There was one problem. Jonah hated Nineveh and the people of the city. So, he fled God's calling by boarding a ship in the opposite direction to Tarshish. But God had a plan for Jonah and Nineveh. So, he sent a storm to get Jonah's attention. The people on the ship threw Jonah into the ocean where he was swallowed by a fish. God eventually released Jonah, but God made his point! When Jonah finally made it to Nineveh, he was obedient and all of Nineveh was saved. Sometimes the storms are used to bring us back to God's designed path for our lives. We can never reach our full potential running away from the place God has called us to be. Adversity has a purpose and work, and we benefit greatly when we understand what God is doing through it.

MAKE IT PERSONAL

- "God as a risk taker" Define a moment when you knew God was taking a risk on you?

  _____

  _____

  _____

- What brand new spiritual experiences create excitement and wonder in your life and are turning out differently than you imagined? What are you doing to press through?

  _____

_____

_____

- Write a few things that God is doing in you to fulfill your calling?

_____

_____

_____

- List one embarrassing moment you had in the wilderness?

_____

_____

- What is a risk God is asking you to take?

_____

_____

_____

- "We benefit greatly when we understand what God is doing" What are some lessons adversity has taught you? Be specific.

_____

_____

_____

- As Christians we are not called to walk alone, who are you walking with in this season?

_____

_____

_____

5

PROTECTING YOUR POTENTIAL

"Sight is a function of the eyes, but
Vision is a function of the heart."

-MYLES MONROE

In the dictionary, the word potential means: "having or showing the capacity to become or develop into something in the future." Your personal potential is something uncultivated and is so valuable you must rise up to protect it at certain seasons of your life. I have learned that if we are not careful and intentional about protecting our potential, we can malfunction and shipwreck along the way. Spiritual growth and success are a journey and I have discovered that there are "snares in the road" that want to disqualify us for God's great plan for our lives. I call these things, "Vision Vandals".

VISION VANDALS

There isn't anything that the enemy can do to defeat you from the outside, defeat is usually an inside job. Nobody is exempt from self-destruction and self-sabotaging their destiny. It is important to be aware of the inner forces that try to limit our potential. There are 4 inner forces in a person's life that if gone unchecked could defeat us personally.

PRIDE

"Pride goes before destruction, and a haughty spirit before a fall. Better to be of a humble spirit with the lowly than to divide the spoil with the proud."

Proverbs 16:18

Why is this an issue? God wants to do His vision His way. We want to do the vision our way. Joseph is a good example that vision and pride don't mix.

1 Peter 18:5-6 says, "Likewise you younger people, submit yourselves to your elders. Yes, all of you be

submissive to one another, and be clothed with humility,
for 'God resists the proud, But gives grace to the humble.'
Therefore humble yourselves under the mighty hand of
God, that He may exalt you in due time..."

When pride steps in,
God steps out!

I want to revisit Joseph for a moment. In the early phases of his life Joseph thought the vision was about him. You know the story, he had a big dream, he had favor from his father, he had a shiny coat, representing his favor and special calling, but he was busy bragging and telling on his brothers, showing the traits of youth and inexperience. So, what do we learn from Joseph's life? When pride steps in, God steps out!

Pride pushed Joseph right out of the presence of God. I know this sounds harsh, but remember, God wants the glory for our lives. God wants every visionary leader to stay under His covering, because vision is a powerful gift from Heaven. Pride pushes a young leader out of the presence of

God and makes us vulnerable to attack. Joseph went from God's Presence, to Pride, to a Pit!

Pride causes good people to walk away from us.

According to this segment of the story there are three things we can learn about pride. Pride causes good people to walk away from us. Joseph suffered from an out of control ego. Ego stands for "Edging God Out." I have discovered that when pride comes in, we are often the last ones to see it, causing for good people who can help us along the way to walk away from us. Pride exposes us to attack. Without God in our lives, we become extra vulnerable. Effectiveness comes from the Lord and we need Him to do what He has called us to do. Pride causes God to have to deal with us. The pit was God's method for dealing with His son, Joseph. What happens to a person who is in a pit? They are surrounded by darkness and closed in and there is only one direction to look and that is UP!

If you are struggling with pride, I have some good news, I have learned through God's mercy, He never moved the dream, but I believe that He strengthened Joseph in His process and ultimately promoted him to the palace.

Compromise

Sinful compromise holds the vision hostage. When sin goes undealt with in a young leader's life, it will eventually stall their purpose. There are things that God doesn't want a person of potential to touch. There are things He wants us to do and things He says, "Don't do that, don't go there, don't touch that," because He is a Father. King Saul compromised and God's favor was eventually removed from his life. Saul failed to follow the instructions of the Lord when he was commanded to destroy Amalek. Saul spared the king and kept some of the spoils.

Sinful compromise holds the vision hostage.

After defeating Jericho miraculously, Joshua and the people of Israel could not defeat the small town of Ai because of Achan's sin. Sin crept into the camp and Israel was drained of its power to take possession of that small town. Lastly, in Numbers 33:55, Israel was commanded to drive out all of the inhabitants of the promised land. Here is a powerful truth. If they did not, God told them that they would be irritants in their eyes and thorns in their side. Friends, obedience brings the victory, compromise brings defeat! God is looking for full obedience. Partial obedience is disobedience.

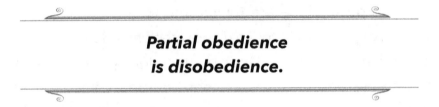

Partial obedience is disobedience.

LAZINESS

Can I be honest with you? The topic of laziness is a personal one for me. What if I were to tell you that before I turned my life over to Jesus, I was probably the laziest person I knew. It is kind of embarrassing looking back today. But the truth is I lived a very uninspired life. I possessed no passion for any cause. I wanted maximum results on minimum effort. I often tell people that when God delivered me from drugs and alcohol, He also delivered me from being lazy. Now I am not ashamed to reveal this about myself for a few reasons, because I have discovered that there are many people in this world who fail to rise up because they lack the personal drive and essential work ethic to succeed.

> ***"Without vision the people perish, but without passion the vision perishes."***

The first thing we should know is that without passion we cannot succeed in life. Passion is a powerful force in anything we set out to do. I have often said, "without vision the people perish, but without passion the vision perishes." Passion must be protected at all costs. Secondly, we should know that God rewards those who are diligent in their work. We are personally rewarded according to our work ethic. Allow me to share two scriptures: Proverbs 12:11 says, "Those who work their land will have abundance of food, but those who chase fantasies have no sense."

Proverbs 20:4 says, "Sluggards don't plow in season, so at harvest time they look and find nothing!"

Here is some simple wisdom that goes a long way. If God has given you a vision, ask the Lord to give you the strength and passion to develop the work ethic required to see that vision come to pass. Align yourself with other hardworking people and stay away from people who waste time and have no purpose in their lives.

FEAR

I know this is a big statement, but it is something I truly believe. The number one reason people never reach their potential is because of fear; the fear of failure, the fear of change, the fear of criticism, the fear of some strange thing happening to them, it goes on and on and on. I want you to know that fear at every level of your life will make or break you spiritually. You see when God calls you to accomplish great things, it can only happen by something called faith. People of faith can see things before they happen. People of faith are willing to stretch into new territory for their lives. People of faith do not shrink back in fear. It is one thing to have a vision or an idea, but if you never stretch out to accomplish it, the idea will only remain a concept.

What is the difference between fear and faith? Fear is a gripping emotion, faith is a releasing emotion. There are two types of people on a roller coaster, those who grip the safety bar as tight as they can and those who throw their hands in the air or to the sky enjoying the ride every step of the way. Faith is not reckless but faith involves trusting God for your future and for your blessings. Fear wants us to grip.

Faith wants us to release. I want to tell you a story about fear. I have personally learned that fear wants to hold onto familiar things from our past.

When my wife and I moved to San Diego to lead the church we have been pastoring for ten years, we entered into a tough situation. A church that was once thriving had shrunken down to maybe seventy-five people on Sunday. They were in danger of losing their very large building and let's just say, people weren't feeling too positive at the time. Many of the people were actually pretty resistant to having new young pastors. And it was tough to find people who were feeling good about the changes. Keep in mind, my wife and I had just released a successful global ministry that we had pioneered for eleven years, and were relocating to a city where we were totally unfamiliar. We were looking for friends. I remember one day a man who had been in the church for a number of years and played guitar on our worship team came up to me after service and said, "Hey I want to give you something." He said, "I want to give you a pool table." Feeling like this was an opportunity to make a new friend and connect with a pillar in the church, I agreed to take the pool table, and besides, who doesn't want a cool pool table in their house? At thirty-one years old, I certainly did.

When the pool table arrived, I made room in the garage of my new house. Because we had just relocated from the East Coast and Los Angeles, I had accumulated a lot for my children - clothes, toys, bikes, reading materials, books, etc. from my office. Let's just say, I had a lot of stuff. But I was excited about the pool table. I pushed all that stuff into the corners of the garage and I went down to the store to buy some new pool cues, racks and all the things to get set up. Once we were ready, I started to have the guys from the church come over to hang out, talk sports, connect and play pool. It was a lot of fun. Just like when you get something brand new. I can still remember whenever we would pull the pool cue back to hit a ball, sometimes we would bump into a box or one of my kid's old bikes. But nevertheless, we used the pool table often, after church on Friday nights and at parties at the house. It was fun to have a pool table. It was a blessing.

But when we hold onto what is old, we can never take possession of what is new.

As time went by and things became busier, I can remember pulling my car into the garage after a long day of church and placing my sermon notes or things I had received through the day on the pool table. After a couple of months of having fun with the table, it actually became a place to put things that weren't being used. I remember I would see coats and jackets, school books, and miscellaneous things on the pool table. I really liked that pool table, we had fun with the guys, we connected around that table, but I remember coming home one day and saying to myself, maybe it's time for the table to go. I picked up the phone and called one of my friends from LA. I offered him the table, he didn't hesitate. Before I could hang up the phone, a U-Haul truck pulled up to my driveway and the pool table was gone! It felt that fast. I remember the next day after the pool table was gone, I felt sad. I looked around the garage at all the stuff I had accumulated on my ministry journeys. Old bikes for the kids, clothes that we didn't wear, books that were given to us by the carload. It dawned on me, "Why didn't I give away or even throw away all of this stuff from my past?" Instead, I gave away a brand-new pool table to hold onto my memories of yesterday. I was so emotionally attached to the clutter, I missed out on a brand-new blessing in my life. Fear wants us to hold on and hold back. When we hold onto what is old, we can never take possession of what is new. A vandal is someone who wants to come in and deliberately destroy your destiny. Be wise, be alert, and be persistent.

MAKE IT PERSONAL

- Vision Vandals; Pride, Compromise, Laziness, Fear. Which is your greatest struggle? What will you do to correct it?

_____

_____

_____

- How do you intend to protect your personal potential?

_____

_____

_____

- Give an example when fear has gripped you in life?

_____

_____

_____

- What are things that fuel your passion? What is your passion?

_____

_____

_____

Personal Application: What will you practically do this week when your vision vandal shows up?

CHAPTER

6

POTENTIAL. GOD'S PRODUCT.

"Someone is sitting in the shade today, because someone planted a tree a long time ago."

-WARREN BUFFETT

Just recently, I was scheduled to have dinner with my daughter Zanelle. She was born during the days when Georgina and I were directing the Urban Training Center in Bridgeport. Today she is a beautiful young woman of nineteen. She just graduated high school and she is very active for God. She is a leader in the youth ministry, she attends San Diego State and works for the San Diego Sheriff's Dept. Let's just say she is a multi-tasker. I sent her a text because I wanted to know where we would be having dinner. In her typical millennial way, she texted me back, "TBD". What does that even mean? TBD means To Be Determined.

A DESTINY TO BE DETERMINED

On this journey, our potential is developed over a lifetime. We must recognize our responsibility is cultivating our potential in the place God has planted us. Truth is, not every person reaches his/her full potential.

> **The richest place in the world is the graveyard.**

I am a firm believer that it is possible to prosper when you are planted in the right ground. We must have a focus and determination when it comes to reaching our potential. You may ask? Is it a contradiction to say that we can be saved and be unproductive? I thought that all believers were productive in the kingdom? The answer is "No". Many are saved and unproductive for God. It has been said, that the richest place in the world is not the US Federal Reserve Bank. The richest place in the world is the graveyard. In the graveyard, there are unfinished projects and unfulfilled dreams. Churches and businesses never built, books never written, places never visited, people never impacted, potential unfulfilled! I know that seems harsh, but it is reality and a person of vision understands the importance of pressing towards his/her vision and developing for God. How do we know someone is being unproductive? I have noticed there are three ways.

"The opportunity of a lifetime must be seized in the lifetime of the opportunity."

Many have time and waste it. Ephesians 5:15 says, Be very careful, then, how you live-not as unwise but as wise, making the most of every opportunity, because the days are evil. Many have opportunities and miss it. Someone once said, "The opportunity of a lifetime must be seized in the lifetime of the opportunity." Unfortunately, doors close for people before they listen to their faith that is saying walk on through. Many have duties and neglect them. Spiritual laziness is a problem for people.

Proverbs 20:4 says, "A sluggard does not plow in season, so at harvest time he looks but finds nothing."

Those who fall into this category lose more than just a blessing; they make a statement about their convictions to the world that is watching them. How does the world see these types of people? Often, they are seen as lacking authenticity. One of the true characteristics of the Christian life is passion. Passion is the fuel that drives our personal development. Passion is something that wakes us up in the morning. It causes us to press with diligence towards God's perfect plan in our lives. Without passion, it is impossible to stay connected to the vine of Christ. If we have been chosen by God we are called to bear much fruit! This is what tells the entire world that we are His disciples.

"When you produce much fruit, you are my true disciples. This brings great glory to my Father."

-John 15:8

There is a parable in the gospel told by Jesus about a fig tree in Luke 13. There was a design for the tree. There was a designation for the tree. There was a disappointment with the tree's progress. There was a "TBD". A destiny to be determined.

What does this parable teach us? It really teaches us three things. First, to recognize the value of time in our lives. It teaches us to recognize the grace of God in our lives. And it teaches us to recognize the responsibility we have to our mission in life. It teaches us to be productive for the Lord. This is a powerful parable and when it comes to this story, I want to bring out 4 D's.

God has a very specific design and plan for your life.

There was a designed plan for the tree. A man had a fig tree, planted in his vineyard. In Luke 13:6 Jesus portrays a landowner who was in possession of a fig tree and a vineyard. How do we know that this tree was there by design? Because, we find that it had been deliberately planted in the vineyard. If we are to look at the original language of this scripture, we can read it this way; The fig tree had been planted within the vineyard, in a most favorable position, by a deliberate act of the owner, in order that he might ultimately enjoy its fruit. I want you to know that God has a very specific design and plan for your life. There are two powerful things we can draw from this parable.

First, we belong to God as His property. We have been purchased by the precious blood of Jesus and as His property, He is within His right to expect fruit from our lives as our owner. Also, we have been positioned for greatness. We have been strategically planted and positioned to bear fruit. The fact that the fig tree was planted in a vineyard, tells us that the soil was the choicest soil that could be found. It was planted with care. In order for that tree to be effectively planted, it would have had to be planted in the corner of the vineyard so that it could be cared for without trampling the other vines.

You see, when God planted us, He planted us in good soil. For many of us, He has strategically and carefully planted us in a good church with good pastors. And, He has positioned us so He can tend to our lives. In other words, we have been set apart for His service. He has carefully placed us to begin to prosper for His purpose. God is well pleased with a church that is willing to be fruitful for His glory. He has not called us to be stagnant, or to be still, He has called us to be fruitful with our vision in mind. Do you consider yourself a fruitful Christian? Are you prospering where you are planted? As the story continues, we find that there was disappointment in the tree.

Luke 13:6-7 says, "He (the owner) went to look for fruit on it, but did not find any. So he said to the man who took care of the vineyard. 'For three years now I've been coming to look for fruit on this fig tree and haven't found any. Cut it down! Why should it use up the soil."

Don't let me lose you here. Stay with me. One purpose dominated the mind of this landowner, that at the appointed time he would be able to enjoy the fruit of this fig tree. The fruit is His purpose and the fruit is His right as owner. The land owner was clearly upset that after all the investment in this fig tree, the care, time and money he had expended upon this tree, he had approached the tree expecting succulent fruit but found none. Here is a valuable question. What does God see when He takes a look at your life? Is your life full of passion? Is your life impacting others when they see your commitment to God? Is there fruit that is causing the vision to advance? Is your life making a difference for God in some area? Is your life contagious? Are you able to say that your life is a fruitful life for God? Can God depend upon you to build His kingdom purpose? What would God see if He were to put your life to the test? We must readily understand that God desires fruit from us. He is looking to and fro looking for those who are living that life of obedience. God help us to be aware!

Friends look at the urgency of God for us to bear much fruit, to be God's product. What did this land owner say?

For three years now I've been coming to this fig tree and haven't found anything. Cut it down!

-Luke 13:7b

Friends, three years was significant because according to horticulture, if a tree did not bear fruit within three years, it was considered unfruitful. Three years of unfruitfulness was the mark of barrenness. The landowner was ready to remove the dead tree and to replace it with a new tree. Even though the tree might have shown signs of hope at times, judgment was upon that tree.

Let's go a little deeper. It was just like Israel's relationship with Christ during the three years of His ministry. At times there seemed to be so much hope, times when the people seemed to be catching it, but then they would immediately revert to their doubt. That is how people of the church can be, you know them. They go through seasons of doing well, only to revert to negativity, fear and doubt until God finally moves His blessings on to others who are willing to produce fruit by Him and for Him. God will not contend forever with the will of men, eventually God will take His blessing and place it on others. Let's not miss our opportunity!

DELAYED JUDGEMENT

Wow! That was intense. Because our potential for personal development is both intense and intentional. The third thing we see in this story is delayed judgment.

Thank God that He is patient with us. This is where we see the grace, mercy and love of Jesus in action for each and every one of us. In Luke 13:8, you can almost hear the throbbing cry of the vine dresser or the intercessor of the tree.

Sir, the man replied, 'Leave it alone for one more year, and I'll dig around it and fertilize it. If it bears fruit next year, fine! If not, then cut it down.'

Luke 13:8

Give the tree one more year! Amazing! Jesus is our heavenly intercessor and this is a picture of Jesus asking for God to give us time to grow and change. Please God give them time. Don't reign your judgment upon the unfruitful of the land, but just give it a little time. This is our opportunity. While Jesus is interceding, you and I must not continue to operate business as usual. This is our opportunity to grow and expand. This is our time to develop our gifts. This is our time to draw closer to God in prayer. This is our time to read and apply His word. This is our time to win souls and to make disciples. This is our time to reach our full potential! We can do it if we work hard and don't give up!

THE VINE DRESSER'S PROMISE

While the owner granted his request, the vine dresser promised to dig around the tree. In other words, for the tree to be fruitful, he had to get to the root of the problem. Is it a lack of prayer? Is it bitterness from past hurts? Is it laziness and a poor work ethic? Is it a rebellious attitude? Is it lack, overall, of spirituality? What is the root of the problem? In order for fruit to spring forth, we must plug into the vine and allow God to dig around our heart. Let God dig out the issues in our lives that hold our destinys back. It can be a painful process, but when you allow God to dig around your heart, your soil becomes more workable for the Master's use.

Jesus spoke of different types of hearts in Mark 4. As the seed was scattered, it fell on different surfaces. Each surface determined whether the seed was planted and whether fruit was born. The vine dresser promised to fertilize the soil around the tree. Why did this tree need fertilizer? Because fertilizer provides the missing elements the tree needs for proper growth. The vine dresser must have felt that if he could provide the missing elements to the tree, then this tree would grow, but fertilizer also produces accelerated growth. Growth would bring great joy to the owner of the tree. Here is an important question when it comes to reaching our full potential.

How does God fertilize us? Here are some things I have learned along the way.

The Word of God is sharp and powerful.

God always uses His word to fertilize our lives. The Word of God is sharp and powerful. It is only the Word of God that can cut us to the heart. God also gives us His Holy Spirit. The Holy Spirit is a teacher, a guide, an encourager. Through the power of the Holy Spirit, we are convicted of the things we read about in the Bible. We are convicted of old behaviors that represent our past. The person of the Holy Spirit helps us to apply all that we learn and ultimately helps us to shape and mold Godly character in our lives. Lastly, I believe that God will use the three P's. People, problems, and places to develop us. This was some of the process God put me through when he fertilized my life. Truthfully, at the time of fertilization it did not feel good. I did not like it. The people weren't nice. The problems were painful, and the places were difficult. But looking back today, I can rejoice and thank

God for those times. They were some of the most exciting and beautiful times because of the purity of hope and our anticipation for the future. Today, I am grateful because as I look back, I can also see how far God has brought us. Leadership is not a destination, it is a journey and we are all still going. It will never end.

Leadership is not a destination it is a journey.

In conclusion, what eventually happened to this tree? There is really no answer. Jesus leaves the ending up to us. It is a message that has no ending. Only an ending TO BE DETERMINED by you and I.

How will you complete this story? Will you become fruitful for God? Will you reach your full potential? Will you rise up and rise over the challenges or will you be replaced by a more willing and fruitful tree in the overall plan of God? It is up to us. It is up to you! But I believe you can do ALL things through Christ who strengthens you. Prosper where you are planted!

Make It Personal

- In your own words, do you think it is a contradiction to say that we can be saved and be unproductive? How do we know someone is being unproductive?

_____

_____

_____

- Luke 13. A destiny to be determined, what does this parable teach us?

_____

_____

_____

- Can God depend upon you to build His kingdom purpose?

_____

_____

_____

- What does God see when He looks at your life? Is your life full of passion? Is your life impacting others?

  _____

  _____

  _____

- How does God fertilize us? (In your own words)

  _____

  _____

  _____

CHAPTER

7

KEEP RISING

"Man cannot aspire if he looks down,
if he is to RISE, he must look up!"

-SAMUEL SMILE

To be a child of God is to embark on a very exciting spiritual journey. We know that our destination is eternal life in Heaven, however Jesus offers us so much more. As we eagerly await His return we also enjoy the many benefits of His kingdom here and now. Jesus said in John 10:10, "The thief does not come except to steal, and to kill and to destroy. I have come that they may have life, and that they may have it more abundantly." The journey is exciting because the possibilities are endless. I've come to find that the abundant life here on earth comes in a very personal and passionate relationship with Jesus. A relationship that is built through a life of prayer, the deep study of God's Word and the passionate service to others, especially to those who are hurting in this world. Our lives make an impact. There is no greater joy in life than to help someone who is in desperate need for change. When you are fully aware of what Christ has done for you, it is a natural desire to reach out to the hurting people of the world and to share with them the very same love you and I have received.

The journey is exciting because the possibilities are endless.

What comes next is a deep desire to grow and develop spiritually for God's glory, to be an example to others and to rise up to our full potential in Christ. A desire to become an effective vessel, a sharp weapon for God has always been a passion of mine. It is not always easy, but we can do it. We know we can do it because of the love and grace of Jesus and because of the people God sends us as partners; they are the ones who believe in us, sharpen us and inspire us for greatness. Our lives become a powerful product of our commitment to Christ and the support of other Godly influences. You see, God desires for each and every person to rise up to become everything He has called them to be. I firmly believe that. There is leadership in all of us. YES, leadership.

There is leadership in all of us.

When we hear something like leadership, we have a tendency to shrink back, because sometimes we can feel inadequate based on our upbringing, or someone else's opinion of us. There is a scripture found in 1 Corinthians 1:27, that has always given me great hope regarding this idea, "But God has chosen the foolish things of the world to put to shame the wise, and God has chosen the weak things of the world to put to shame the things that are mighty". This scripture gives me hope because there have been many times in my life when I have felt unworthy and inadequate. Times when I felt like I did not measure up. Truth is: I have never been anyone's first choice. I fully understand rejection. I have felt overlooked at times. I came from a broken family. I had teachers in school who looked down upon me. I wasn't the best looking in school. I wasn't the most athletic. I wasn't the most affluent or connected person. It seems like some people have to work harder than others. However, I was chosen by God at nineteen years old. I heard His voice in my heart calling me to do His work. I began to realize that when a person is chosen by God and is willing to totally commit to God's plan, then the past is forgiven and forgotten, things are made brand new and the limits are removed! The truth is, each one of us is God's first choice!

We will lead our families.
We will lead in our communities
and lead at home.

When I speak of leadership in our lives, I am not only speaking of the fact that God desires to shape us into powerful leaders in His church, but He also desires to shape us into people who will effectively impact and inspire our surroundings for the good. We will lead our families. We will lead in our communities and lead at home. We will help to build the ministry. We will answer the call. Some will build powerful businesses, develop ideas to improve people's lives, improve their communities and impact people personally. As we develop our personal potentials, God expands our influence for the good of others. It is very exciting to be used by God in this way and many doors begin to open for us as a result.

Today, I am grateful for the doors and opportunities that have been opened to my wife and I. God has placed us in what I believe to be one of the greatest ministries in the world, the ministry of Victory Outreach International. Together we are blessed to serve some of the greatest people in the world. We pastor a thriving and exciting church in San Diego, CA. We aspire to fulfill a God-given vision that calls us to reach the inner cities of the world with the message, hope and plan of Jesus Christ. Our work is challenging but extremely fulfilling. We have had the opportunity to literally see thousands of people who come from the darkest places of sin, rise up to become mighty in the Kingdom of God. People who were once lost and bound by drugs, alcohol, depression, fear, anger, brokenness, abandonment; today are not only successful and productive contributors to family and society, but community leaders, business owners and powerful ministers of the gospel. They are what we call "Treasures Out of Darkness".

After twenty-five years of ministry, I reflect on a young man who was broken and lost. Because of the grace and mercy of God, my wife Georgina and I have worked with some amazing people. We have experienced many great things in our lives. In our twenty-two years of marriage we have traveled and ministered in twenty countries. We are raising four wonderful children and we are building a thriving young church in San Diego, CA, Victory Outreach San Diego. We are excited about working with people, whether they are struggling with drugs or graduating from college, building businesses or rebuilding their lives, leading their families or pastoring their churches. We are passionate for God and passionate for people. We have dedicated our lives to helping others win! We are committed to the process of discipleship and are constantly striving to grow and learn ourselves. We have not arrived and we remain excited about what God has next. I want to leave you with some important keys or tips to reaching your full potential.

Number #1

Submit to God's plan for your life. Commit to the journey of spiritual growth and development. It is not always easy, but it always brings great results. Be patient. Be kind. Be committed. Remain humble in all that you do.

Number #2

Partner with people of like mind and like heart. Make sure you are aligned with God's word, your pastor and spiritual leaders, and people of the like. If you want to be an eagle, hang out with eagles! God's people are a special people on the earth. Partner with them in all you do. Proverbs 13:20, "Walk with the wise and become wise, for the companion of fools will be destroyed."

If you want to be an eagle, hang out with eagles!

Number #3

Challenge yourself personally. Do something you have never done before. When was the last time you did something for the first time? Don't be afraid to step out in some area that God is leading you. Take the challenges and don't be afraid to fail. If you get knocked down once, get up and try again. Life favors the bold! Victory is guaranteed to those who will not quit!

Number #4

Take off the limits. Forget the past, press towards the future. Get around the people who truly believe in you and encourage you. Get around the people who are moving forward. Get around the people who are committed to God's plan in their lives. Ask them questions. Be a learner at all times. Get into the rooms where you aren't the smartest person there. There are no limits for a learner.

In conclusion, that's the pure beauty of spiritual development. We never fully arrive. We only continue to rise! With every obstacle and every disappointment comes a new opportunity and a new miracle to be released and a new victory on the horizon, which brings me to number 5.

Number #5

As the great Prime Minister Winston Churchill once told a graduating college class, "Never give up! Never give up! Never give up!" And as he walked off that stage after his extremely short speech, I conclude by echoing the thoughts given that day, "Never give up. Never give up. Never give up." Keep rising!

MAKE IT PERSONAL

Submit to God's plan for your life

Partner with people of like-mind

Challenge yourself personally

Take off the limits.

Never Give Up!

Using the 5 Keys mentioned in this chapter,

In one year, what are some personal goals you want to see accomplished in your life?

CPSIA information can be obtained
at www.ICGtesting.com
Printed in the USA
LVHW030828110320
649571LV00004BA/123

9 781949 758344